Lidia Kosk

Nine Poems in Nine Incarnations

Lidia Kosk

NINE POEMS IN NINE INCARNATIONS

Selected and Edited by Danuta E. Kosk-Kosicka

It is a good time for translations.
To spread hope and understanding.
To make connections.

LOCH RAVEN PRESS SYKESVILLE, MD 2026

Printed in the United States of America

Cover Art: Painting by Danuta E. Kosk-Kosicka, titled "Under One Sun." Back cover photo of Lidia Kosk is by Andrzej J. Kosicki.

Cover and book design: Danuta E. Kosk-Kosicka and Jim Doss

ISBN 979-8-9905505-8-2

Loch Raven Press
140 Milrey Drive, Suite L
Sykesville, MD 21784

Illustrations to the Poems:

"From the Window of My Apartment" — photo by Lidia Kosk
"At the Water Spring" — photo by Danuta E. Kosk-Kosicka
"Listening to Jazz" — photo by Paweł Mizgalewicz
"Curious About the World" — photo by Grażyna Kosk-Wiśniewska
"Flower in Your Hair" — drawing by Bohdan Butenko (from Lidia Kosk's book *Liście na wiatr*)
"The Beach at Santa Cruz" — photo by Danuta E. Kosk-Kosicka
"Before a Human Killed With a Human" — photo collage by Danuta E. Kosk-Kosicka
"Awareness" — photo by Danuta E. Kosk-Kosicka
"Settles in the Heart" — photo by Paweł Mizgalewicz

Lidia Kosk

NINE POEMS IN NINE INCARNATIONS

Selected and Edited by Danuta E. Kosk-Kosicka

It is a good time for translations.
To spread hope and understanding.
To make connections.

Each Poem Appears in Nine Consecutive Languages:

English — translation by Danuta E. Kosk-Kosicka
Polish — original version written by Lidia Kosk
Russian — translation by Natalia Romanova
Italian — translation by Sabine Pascarelli
Spanish — translation by Patricia Bejarano Fisher
French — translation by Keith Cohen
German — translation by Peter Beicken
Finnish — translation by Irmeli Kuehnel
Hungarian — translation by Paul Sohar

Table of Contents

POEM ONE

POEM TWO

POEM THREE

POEM FOUR

POEM FIVE

POEM SIX

POEM SEVEN

POEM EIGHT

POEM NINE

POEM ONE

From the Window of My Apartment

Above the apartment house,
whose windows exchange looks with mine,
the moon got stuck
among the rocks and boulders of clouds.
He kept hanging there, stubbornly,
until I forgot that I had broken with him
permanently.
Until I forgot that my soul
did not sing anymore,
until all of me was a song.

Z okna mojego mieszkania

Nad domem naprzeciwko,
co oknami patrzy ku memu oknu,
zawiesił się księżyc,
wśród skał i kamieni z obłoków.
I wisiał długo, wytrwale,
aż zapomniałam, że z nim zerwałam
na stałe.
Aż zapomniałam, że w duszy
już tak dawno brak grania,
aż cała byłam z zapamiętania.

Из окна моей квартиры

Над домом напротив,
чьи окна глядятся в мои,
в небе месяц повис
среди скал и камней облаков.
Он упрямо и долго висел,
пока я не забыла, что с ним
порвала навсегда.
Пока я не забыла что нет
песни в сердце моем,
пока все во мне песней не стало.

Dalla Finestra del mio Appartamento

Sopra la palazzina,
le cui finestre scambiano sguardi con le mie,
la luna venne incastrata
tra rocce e amassi di nuvole.
Ci restò appesa cocciutamente,
finché dimenticai di aver rotto con lei
per sempre.
Finché dimenticai che l'anima mia non cantava più,
finché tutto di me era un canto.

Desde mi ventana

En lo alto del edificio de apartamentos
cuyas ventanas se miran con las mías
se ha quedado atascada la luna
entre rocas y cúmulos de nubes.
Se quedó allí, insistente,
hasta que olvidé que habíamos roto
para siempre.
Hasta que olvidé que mi alma
había dejado de cantar,
hasta que yo toda fui canción.

Par la fenêtre de mon appartement

Au-dessus de l'immeuble,
dont les fenêtres échangent des regards avec les miens,
la lune s'est coincée
parmi les roches et les rochers de nuages.
Elle n'arrêtait pas de traîner là, obstinément,
jusqu'à ce que j'ai oublié que j'avais rompu avec elle,
définitivement.
Jusqu'à ce que j'ai oublié que mon âme
ne chantait plus,
jusqu'à ce que tout en moi était une chanson.

Vom Fenster meiner Wohnung

Über dem Wohnhaus,
dessen Fenster mit mir Blicke tauschen,
ist der Mond eingeklemmt
zwischen Felsen und Bergen von Wolken.
Da hängt er fest, störrisch,
bis ich vergaß, dass ich mich entzweit hatte mit ihm
auf immer.
Bis ich vergaß, dass meine Seele
nicht mehr sang,
bis ich ganz Gesang ward.

Huoneistoni Ikkunasta

Kerrostalon yläpuolella,
jonka ikkunat vaihtavat katsonsa kanssani
kuu on juutunut
kivisten ja kivilohkareiden pilvien keskellä.
Hän roikkui siellä, itsepäisesti,
kunnes unohdin etta olin lopettanut hänen kanssa
lopullisesti.
Kunnes unohdin sieluni
ei laulannut enään,
kunnes kaikki sielussani oli laulu.

Lakásom ablakából

Afelett a bérház felett,
aminek az ablakai szemeznek az enyémmel,
a hold megrekedt
a felhők kövei és sziklái között.
Ott kapaszkodott, konokul,
addig amíg elfeljettem, hogy már elhagytam
örökre.
Addig amíg elfelejtettem hogy a lelkem
soha többé nem énekel,
addig amíg egy ének lett belőlem.

POEM TWO

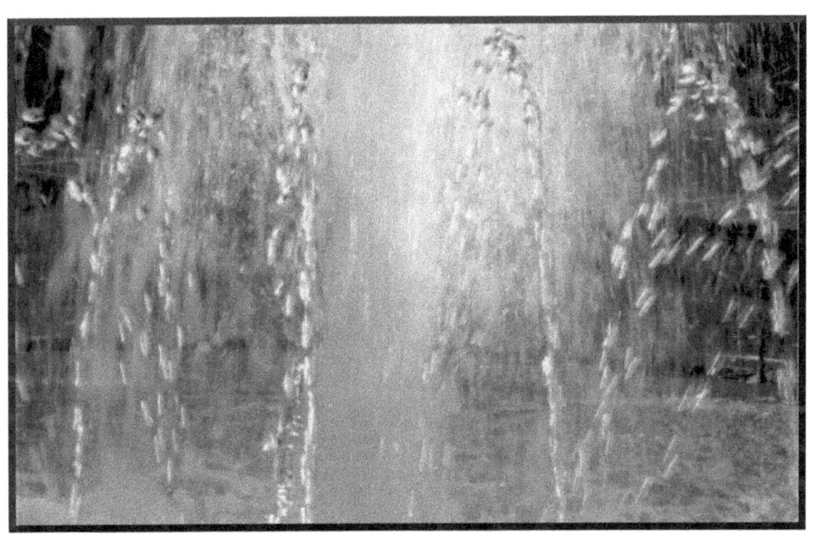

At the Water Spring

I met you, Maria
at a pulsating
little water spring
my pail waiting
to be filled

I kept meeting you, Maria
whenever I needed
water from the spring
when unsure I kept
finding it pulsating
in spite of everything

and after years
thirsting for its water
if I traverse the distance
find the overgrown path
and the hidden
water's eye

the source
not dried out
I will meet you there, Maria

Spotkanie przy źródle

Spotkałam cię Mario
gdy z maleńkiego oczka
pulsującej wody czerpałam
garnuszkiem
puste wiaderko obok
oczekiwało napełnienia

spotykałam cię Mario
ilekroć potrzebowałam
zaczerpnąć wody
ze źródełka
gdy niepewna znajdowałam
je wciąż pulsujące

a po latach
gdy zapragnę jego wody
i pokonam zaistniałą odległość
jeśli znajdę porosłą chaszczami
ścieżkę
do źródełka

jeżeli nie wyschło
spotkam cię tam Mario

Встреча у родника

Я встретила тебя Мария
у маленького родника
когда черпала кувшином
пульсирующую воду
пустое ведро рядом
ожидало наполнения

Я встречала тебя Мария
когда мне было нужно
зачерпнуть воды
из родника
когда неуверенная
я всегда находила его пульс

Если через годы
и расстояния
я опять возжажду его воды
и найду заросшую тропинку
к его маленькому глазку
если он еще не высох
я встречу тебя там Мария

Alla Fonte

Ti incontrai, Maria
a una piccola
pulsante fonte d'acqua
il mio secchio pronto
d'essere riempito

Continuai a incontrarti, Maria
ogni volta avevo bisogno di
acqua dalla fonte
quando ero insicura, la
trovai pulsante
nonostante tutto

e dopo anni
di sete per la sua acqua
se percorro la distanza
trovo il sentiero ricoperto
e lì nascosto, l'occhio
dell'acqua

la sorgente
non prosciugata
là t'incontrerò, Maria

Al pie del manantial

Te conocí, María
al pie de un sonoro
manantial
con mi balde a la espera
para llenarlo.

Volví a encontrarte, María
cada vez que iba a buscar
el agua de la fuente
cuando insegura la hallaba
aún vibrante
a pesar de todo

y tras años
de vivir sedienta de su agua
si atravieso esa distancia
encuentro el sendero enmarañado
y oculto
el ojo del agua

la fuente
no se ha secado
allí te encontraré, María

A la source d'eau

Je t'ai rencontrée, Maria
à une petite source d'eau
palpitante
mon sceau attendant
à être rempli

je n'arrêtais pas de te rencontrer, Maria
à chaque fois que j'avais besoin
d'eau de la source
lorsqu'incertaine
je la trouvais toujours palpitante
malgré tout

et après des années
assoiffée pour ses eaux
si je traverse la distance
retrouve le chemin envahi d'herbes
et l'œil caché
de l'eau

la source
ne s'étant pas desséchée
je t'y rencontrerai, Maria

An der Quelle

Ich traf dich, Maria
an der kleinen
sprudelnden Quelle
bercit meinen Eimer
zu füllen

Ich traf dich, Maria
immer wenn ich
das Quellwasser brauchte,
auch wenn unsicher
fand ich es sprudeln
trotz alledem.

und nach Jahren
durstig nach ihrem Wasser
wenn ich aus der Ferne kam
fand ich den überwachsenen Pfad
und versteckt
das Auge des Wassers

die Quelle
nicht versiegt
dort treff ich dich wieder, Maria

Vesilähteellä

Tapasin sinut, Maria
pienen sykkivän
veden lähteellä
oma ämpärini odottaen
että täyttäisin sen

Tapasin sinut usein, Maria
aina kun tarvitsin
vettä vesilähteestä
kun olin epävarma
löysin sen aina sykkivänä
kaikesta huolimatta

ja monen vuoden perästä
janoisin sitä vettä
jos kuljin sitä etäisyyttä
löydän umpeen kasvanut polun
ja veden
salaisen silmän

tämä vedenlähde
ei ole kuivunut
Tapaan sinut siellä, Maria

A forrásnál

Találkoztam veled, Maria,
egy kis prüszkölő
forrásnál
a vödröm
feltöltve

továbbra is talákoztam veled, Maria,
amikor viz kellett
a forrásból
bizonytalanul is én
prüszkölve találtam rá
mindennek dacára

évek után is
a vizet kivánva
ha áthidalom a távolságot
rátalálok a benőtt ösvényre
és a rejtett viz
szemére

a forrás
nem apadt el
találkozok még ott veled, Maria

POEM THREE

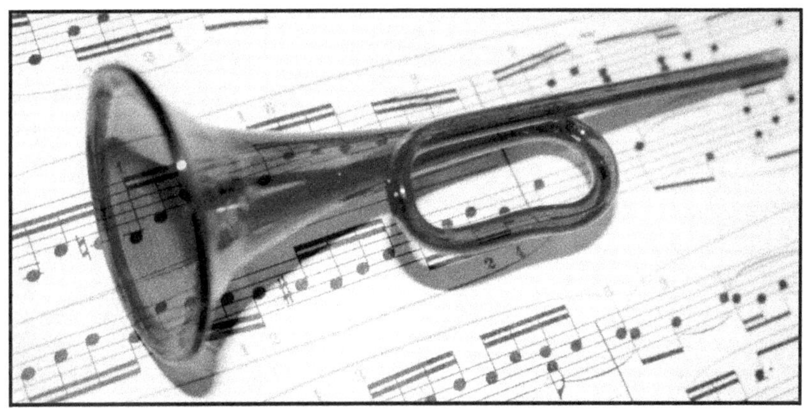

Listening to Jazz

in the midst of chaos
I write down
life
on the table of thoughts

wind blows
snaps up time
splits happenings
into notes

I persist in the sound

Słuchając jazzu

w środku chaosu
zapisuję
na stoliku myśli
życie

przeleciał wiatr
porwał czas
rozsypał zdarzenia
na nuty

w dźwięku trwam

Слушая джаз

среди хаоса
на мысли стол
записываю
жизнь

ветра порыв
время порвал
рассыпал событья
на ноты

в звуке живу

Ascoltando Jazz

nel mezzo del caos
imprimo
la vita
sulla tavola dei pensieri

soffia il vento
acchiappa il tempo
scinde eventi
in note

persisto nel suono

Oyendo Jazz

inmersa en el caos
escribo
vida
sobrc la mesa
de las cavilaciones

sopla el viento
se lleva el tiempo
quiebra en notas
los eventos

persisto en el sonido

Écouter le jazz

au milieu de chaos
j'écris
la vie
sur la table des pensées

le vent souffle
saisit le temps
fend les événements
en notes

je persiste dans le son

Beim Anhören von Jazz

mitten im Chaos
schreib ich
das Leben
auf die tabula rasa des Geistes

Wind geht
schnappt sich die Zeit
spaltet in Noten
was geschieht

Ich verweile im Klang

Jazzia kuuntelemassa

kaoksen keskellä
Kirjoitan
elämästä
ajatuksen pöydällä

tuuli puhaltaa
näpsähtää aikaa
halkaisee tapahtumia
huomautuksiin

pysyn äänessä

Jazz zenét hallgatva

Káos közepette
én megírom
az életet
a gondolatok asztalán

szél fuj
felkapja az időt
felaprítja az eseményeket
hangjegyekre

én megmaradok a hangban

POEM FOUR

Curious about the World

And if I am given the chance
again and once again
to look at the marvel of this world
through eyelashes, like petals
of an apple flower

again and once again
to taste the juicy fruit
imbued in human history
of climbing, reaching up

again and once again
I will reach up
curious about the world
I have not learned enough

Ciekawa świata

A jeżeli będzie mi dane
jeszcze i jeszcze raz
popatrzeć na cud świata
tęczówkami szypułek
okolonych rzęsami płatków
kwiatu jabłoni

jeszcze i jeszcze raz
skosztować soczystego owocu
nasyconego historią człowieka
wspinającego się, dążącego

jeszcze i jeszcze raz
będę się wspinać
ciekawa świata
którego nie zdążyłam poznać

Увлеченная миром

И ежели мне даровано
снова и снова
смотреть
сквозь яблоневые лепестки ресниц
на это чудо
имя которому мир

снова и снова
вкушать сочный плод
насыщенный историей человека
восходящего, устремленного вверх

то снова и снова
вверх буду стремиться
увлеченная миром
что я не успела познать

Incuriosita del Mondo

E se avessi l'occasione
di nuovo e ancora una volta
di guardare le meraviglie di questo mondo
attraverso le ciglia, come petali
d'un fiore di melo

di nuovo e ancora una volta
assaggiare la frutta succosa
imbevuta della storia umana
d'arrampicarsi, d'allungare le braccia

di nuovo e ancora una volta
allungo le braccia
curiosa per il mondo
non ho imparato abbastanza

Curiosa sobre el mundo

Y si tengo la suerte
una y otra vez
de contemplar la maravilla de este mundo
a través de pestañas entreabiertas, como pétalos
de flor de manzano

una y otra vez
de gustar la jugosa fruta
saturada de historia humana
de escalar, de alcanzar

una y otra vez
alzaré los brazos
curiosa sobre el mundo
aún no me basta lo que he aprendido

Curieuse du monde

Et si on me donne l'occasion
Encore et une fois encore
De regarder le miracle de ce monde
A travers les cils, comme des pétales
D'une fleur de pommier

Encore et une fois encore
Goûter le fruit juteux
Imprégnée par l'histoire humaine
De grimper, de tendre la main

Encore et une fois encore
Je lèverai le bras
Curieuse du monde
Je n'en ai pas assez appris

Gespannt auf die Welt

Und wenn es mir gegeben
wieder und wieder
das Wunder der Welt zu sehen
durch die Wimpern, wie durch Blütenblätter
einer Apfelblüte

wieder und wieder
die süße Frucht zu kosten
durchtränkt von der Geschichte
der Menschen die streben und steigen

wieder und wieder
will ich ergreifen
gespannt auf die Welt
was ich noch nicht begriffen

Utelias maailmasta

Ja jos minulle annetaisi mahdollisuuden
jällen ja vielä kerran
katsoa maailman ihmeitä
läpi silmäripsien
kuin omenapuun
terälehdet

jällen ja vielä kerran
maistaa mehukasta hedelmää
joka on imeytynyt ihmishistoriaan
kiipeilystä, ulosnousustа

jällen ja vielä kerran
aion päästä ylös
utelias maailmasta
en ole oppinut tarpeeksi

Kiváncsi a világra

És ha nekem jut az hogy
újra és újra
e világ csodáját nézzzem
almavirág szirmaihoz hasonló
szempillákon át

hogy ujra és ujra
izlelnjem a zaftos gyümölcsöt
ami át van itatva a felfele való
törekvés emebri történelmével

újra és újra
felkapaszkodok
kiváncsian a világra
amiről nem tudok eleget

POEM FIVE

Flower in Your Hair

My city—
    so sad today
with faces of people
    who follow
the disfigured reflections
    of intents
Girl—
    May-girl
so good that you have
    pinned a flower in your hair
for a rendezvous
    with your May paramour
in the romantic
    spring forest
He will
    return with you
back to the city
    unlike the grandfathers
who had to hide
    in the forest
Their faces veiled
    in failed choices
chiseled in stone
    time dusted
bestow
    sadness on the streets
Streets of my city—
    change!
Girl—so good
    that you have
a flower in your hair

Kwiat we włosach

Moje miasto
    dziś takie smutne
twarzami ludzi
    podążających
za zniekształconym
    odbiciem celu
Dziewczyno
    majowa dziewczyno
dobrze, że wpięłaś
    kwiat we włosy
na spotkanie
    z majowym kochankiem
w wiosennym
    romantycznym lesie
Twój chłopiec wróci z tobą
    do domu
las nie służy już
    za schronienie
    jak waszym dziadkom—
to ich twarze w woalkach
    z nietrafionych wyborów
kamienne
    poszarzałe czasem
składają się
    na smutek ulic
Ulico mojego miasta
    zmień się
Dziewczyno, dobrze
    że wpięłaś kwiat

Цветок в волосах

Город мой
    сегодня печален
грустны лица
    его жителей
влекомых
    искаженными тенями
Ой ты девушка
    девушка майская
хорошо что ты вплела
    цветок в волосы
для свидания
    с майским возлюбленным
в романтичном
    весеннем лесу
Твой парень
    вернется с тобою домой
лес не служит уже
    укрытием
как вашим дедам--
    это их каменные лица
под покровом
    неверных решений
запыленые временем наводят грусть
    на улицы города
Улицы моего города
    преобразитесь
Девушка хорошо что у тебя
    в волосах цветок

Un Fiore nei tuoi Capelli

La mia città—
    così triste oggi
con le facce della gente
    che segue
i riflessi sfigurati
    di intenti
Fanciulla—
    fanciulla di maggio
hai fatto bene a mettere
    un fiore nei capelli
per il rendezvous
    col tuo amante di maggio
nella romantica
    primaverile foresta
Lui
    tornerà con te
nella città
    non come i nonni
costretti a nascondersi
    nella foresta
I loro visi velati
    da scelte sbagliate
scolpiti nella pietra
    impolverati dal tempo
conferiscono
    tristezza alle strade
Strade della mia città—
    cambiate!
Fanciulla—bene che
    tu abbia
un fiore nei capelli

Una flor en el pelo

Mi ciudad—
    hoy tan triste
con rostros de gentes
    que siguen
los torcidos reflejos
    de intenciones
Mocita —
    mocita de mayo
qué bien que te hayas puesto
    una flor en el pelo
para la cita
    con tu amante de mayo
en el ensueño
    del bosque en primavera
El
    volverá contigo
de nuevo a la ciudad
    no como los abuelos
que debieron esconderse
    en el bosque
Sus rostros velados
    en fallidas opciones
cincelados en piedra
    por el polvo del tiempo
entristecen
    las calles
Calles de mi ciudad—
    ¡es hora de cambiar!
Mocita
    qué bueno que lleves
esa flor en el pelo

Fleur dans tes cheveux

Ma ville—
    si triste aujourd'hui
aux figures des gens
    qui suivent
les reflets défigurés
    de buts
Fille—
    fille de mai
que c'est bien
    cette fleur
que tu as épinglée dans tes cheveux
pour un rendez-vous
    chez ton amant de mai
dans la forêt printanière
    romantique
Il retournera
    avec toi
en ville
    pas comme les grand pères
qui devaient se cacher
    dans la forêt
Les figures voilées
    par des choix échoués
ciselées en pierre
    saupoudrées par le temps
Accorde
    la tristesse aux rues
La rue de ma ville—
    change !
Fille—que c'est bien
    cette fleur
que tu as épinglée dans tes cheveux

Deine Blume im Haar

Meine Stadt—
heute so traurig
mit den Gesichtern der Leute
die folgen
den entstellten Reflexionen
von Anliegen
Mädchen—
Mai-Mädchen
wie schön dass du gesteckt hast
eine Blume ins Haar
für ein Stelldichein
mit deinem Mai-Geliebten
im romantischen
Frühlingswald
Er wird
mit dir zurückgehen
in die Stadt
anders als die Großväter
die sich verbergen mussten
im Wald
ihre Gesichter markiert
von verfehlter Wahl
in Stein gemeißelt
verstaubt von der Zeit
verleihen
den Straßen Traurigkeit
Ihr Straßen meiner Stadt—
werdet anders!
Mädchen—wie schön
dass du gesteckt hast
deine Blume ins Haar

Kukka hiuksissa

Kaupunkini—
        niin surullinen tänään
ihmisten kasvoilla
        jotka seuraavat
vääristyneitä heijastuksia
        aikeista
Tyttö
        toukokuun tyttö
niin hyvä että olet
        kiinnittänyt kukan hiuksiinsa
tapaamiselle
        toukokuun kultaseni kanssa
romanttisessa
        kevä metsässä
hän aikoo
        palata luoksesi
takaisin kaupunkiin
        toisin kuin isoisät
jotka piti piiloutua
        metsään
heidän kasvonsa verhottu
        epäonnistuneista valinnoista
veistetty kiveen
        ajan pölyämä
lahjoittaneet
        surua kaduille—
vaithtelua!
tyttö—niin hyvä
        että sinulla on
kukka hiuksissa

Virág a hajadban

Városom—
oly szomorú ma
az arcoktól amik
követik az eltozult
szándékok
tükörképeit
Kislány—
májusi lány
milyen jó hogy egy virágot
tüztél a hajadba
randira menet
a májusi szeretőddel
a romantikus
tavaszi erdőbe
Ő majd
visszamegy veled
a városba
nem úgy mint a nagyapák
akiknek az erdőben
kellett rejtőzködniük
Arcukat elrontott
választás takarta
köbe faragva
az idő porában
az áraszt
szomort az utcákba
Városom utcái—
újjuljakot meg!
Kislány—milyen jó
hogy virág

POEM SIX

The Beach at Santa Cruz

She steps out from the shadow
of a tree looming over the beach
when the tide begins to ebb
she slides into the ocean
her shawl fluttering like a sail
suddenly tangles in the horizon
eyes lose control
the distance quivers
foaming waters roar
her dress clinging to her body
she rides on the crest of the wave
returning to the shore
her dripping feet
moisten the sand

sun rays drink
moisture off the footprints
more and more dry sand
sifts through the toes
sifting
now the sand sifting is
not only for myself

I take a fistful of sand
from the far away beach at Santa Cruz

Na plaży w Santa Cruz

pojawiła się w cieniu drzewa
zagarniającym plażę
i wraz z odpływem
zsunęła się do oceanu
jej szal zatrzepotał jak żagiel
nagle zaplątał się w horyzont
wzrok utracił kontrolę
rozdygotana dal ruszyła
zaszumiały spienione grzywy fal
w oblepiającej ciało sukni
galopowała na grzbiecie
powracającej do brzegu wody
ociekającymi stopami
zamoczyła piasek

słoneczne promienie spijają
wilgoć mokrych śladów
coraz więcej suchego piasku
przesypuje się przez palce stóp
przesypywanie
teraz będę to czynić
nie tylko za siebie

nabieram pełną garść piasku
na dalekiej plaży w Santa Cruz

На пляже в Санта Круз

Она вышла из тени дерева
что раскинуло ветви на пляже
и бесшумно скользнула в воду
в отбегающую волну
ее хлопавшая как парус
шаль запуталась в горизонте
и пропала в дрожащей дали
в гриве пены и реве волн
вдруг на гребне белом возникла
в облегающем тело платье
устремилась с приливом к суше
замочила ногами песок

мокрый след осушило солнце
выпив влагу своими лучами
стало больше песка сухого
просеваться сквозь пальцы ног
просевание
не за себя лишь
я теперь это буду делать

горсть песка набираю на пляже
у далекого Санта Круз

La Spiaggia di Santa Cruz

Ella passa dall'ombra di un
albero che incombe sulla spiaggia
quando la marea comincia a rifluire
scivola nell'oceano
il suo scialle che svolazza come una vela
s'attorciglia improvvisamente all'orizzonte
gli occhi perdono il controllo
la distanza freme
la spumeggiante acqua ruggisce
il suo vestito aderisce al corpo
lei cavalca la cresta dell'onda
ritorna alla riva
i suoi piedi bagnati
inumidiscono la sabbia

i raggi del sole bevono
l'umidità dalle sue impronte
più e più sabbia secca
passa dalle dita dei piedi
passa al setaccio
ora la sabbia che passa al setaccio
non è solo per me

prendo una manciata di sabbia
dalla lontana spiaggia di Santa Cruz

La playa en Santa Cruz

Surge de la sombra
de un árbol que se alza sobre la playa
cuando la marea comienza a bajar
se desliza entre las aguas del océano
su chal ondulando como una vela
de repente se enreda en el horizonte
se descontrolan los ojos
tiembla la distancia
rugen las aguas encrespadas
con el traje pegado al cuerpo
cabalga sobre la cresta de la ola
y regresa a la playa
sus pies empapados
mojan la arena

los rayos del sol se beben
la humedad de las pisadas
más y más arena seca
se filtra entre sus dedos
filtrando
filtrar arena ahora
ya no es sólo para mí

me llevo un puñado de arena
de la lejana playa en Santa Cruz

La Plage à Santa Cruz

Elle émerge de l'ombre
d'un arbre qui se dresse sur la plage
quand la marée commence à refluer
elle se glisse dans l'océan
son châle flottant comme un voile
s'enchevêtre tout d'un coup dans l'horizon
les yeux perdent contrôle
la distance frissonne
les eaux écumantes rugissent
la robe se cramponnant à son corps
elle se perd dans la crête de la vague
retournant sur la côte
ses pieds ruisselants
mouillent la sable

rayons de soleil boivent
l'humidité des empreintes
de plus en plus de sable desséchée
coule en un filet des doigts de pied
tamisant
maintenant la sable tamisant n'est pas
seulement pour moi

j'emmène une poignée de sable
de la plage lointaine à Santa Cruz

Am Strand von Santa Cruz

Sie kommt hervor aus dem Schatten
eines über den Strand ragenden Baumes
wenn die Ebbe beginnt
sie gleitet ins Meer
ihr Schal flattert wie ein Segel
plötzlich verworren am Horizont
schwindende Augen
verschwimmende Ferne
schäumende Wasser brausen
ihr Kleid hängt am Körper
sie reitet auf dem Wellenkamm
zurück ans Ufer
ihre triefenden Füße
benetzen den Sand

die Strahlen der Sonne
saugen das Nass aus den Fußabdrücken
immer mehr trockener Sand
sickert durch die Zehen
sickert
jetzt sickert der Sand
nicht nur für mich

ich nehm eine Handvoll Sand
vom fernen Strand bei Santa Cruz

Santa Cruzin ranta

Hän astuu pois puun varjosta
joka hähmöttää yli rantaa
kun vuorovesi alkaa vähetä
hän liekuu valtamereen
hänen huivi lepattaa kuin purje
yhtäkkiä sotkeutuu horisonttiin
silmät menettäävät hallinsa
etäisyys värähtyy
vahtoiset vedet ulvoo
hänen mekko takertuu vartalluunsa
hän ratsastaa allon selällä
palatean rannikkoon
jalkansa tiputaen vetta
kostuttaen hiekkaa

auringon säteet juovat
kosteutta pois jalanjäljiltä
enemmän ja enemmän kuivaa hiekkaa
seuloa varpaitten läpi
nyt hiekkaa seuloo
ei vain minulle

otan hiekkaa nyrkiini
kaukaa Santa Cruzin rannalta

Santa Cruz strandja

Kilép a rpart felett imbolyogó
fa árnyékából
s az apállyal
belemerül az oceánba
szines sálja lobog mint egy vitorla
gabalyog hirtelen a láthatáron
a szemek hatástalanok
a távolsag ingatag
moralylik a habzó viz
a szoknya a testhez ragad
o most már a hullám taralyán nyargal
a partra visszatérve
vizes lábával
megnedvesiti a homkot

a napsugár felissza
a nedvet a lábnyomokról
több és több száraz homok
szitál a lábujjak között
szitálva
most a homok szitál
nem csak nekem

én elhozok egy maréknyi homokot
Santa Cruz távoli strandjáról

POEM SEVEN

Before a Human Killed With a Human

Spills of redness saturated
bandages of clouds
and paled uncovering
a big shield of Sun
The brightness captured our plane

Suddenly it waned
hid behind the falling wall
of indigo clouds driven in
by the last ray
Silent moment of darkness fell

We crossed the threshold
gold-saturated shimmering dawn
dissolved uncovering
the big shield of Sun
It permeated the windows of the plane

The dream that didn't make it
slipped down the ball of Earth
between the red and the gold
of sunset and sunrise
A new ordinary day was born

before a human killed with a human
planes and buildings
full of humans

September 2001

Nim człowiek człowiekiem zamordował

Rozlała się czerwień
nasączyła bandaże obłoków
i blednąc odsłoniła
wielką tarczę Słońca
Chwyta blaskiem mój powietrzny statek

Lecz nagle przygasa
kryje się za opadającą ścianę
chmur zagarniając granat
ostatnim promieniem
Zapada cichy moment ciemności

Przekroczyliśmy próg
nasączył się złotem drgający świt
i rzednąc odsłonił
wielką tarczę Słońca
Wypełniła okna samolotu

Sen który nie zdążył
ześlizgnął się po kulistej ziemi
między czerwień i złoto
zachodu i wschodu
Narodził się nowy zwyczajny dzień

nim człowiek człowiekiem zamordował
samoloty i domy
pełne ludzi

wrzesień 2001

До того как убил человек человеком

Разлилась краснота
пропитала бинты облаков
и поблекнув открыла
диск огромного Солнца
Ловит блеском воздушный корабль

Вдруг тускнеет
последним лучом
синеву поглотив исчезает
за густою стеной облаков
Тихий миг темноты

За порогом
дрожащий рассвет
пропитавшийся золотом тает
перед диском огромного Солнца
Что собою наполнило окна

Сон начавшийся было
скользнул по круглой земле
между золотом утра
и багрянцем заката
День обычный родился

до того как убил человек человеком
самолеты и дома
полные людей

Сентябрь 2001

Prima che un Uomo uccidesse con un Uomo

Traboccanti rossastre fascie
di nuvole saturate
e schiarite svelano
un grande scudo di Sole
La luminosità catturò il nostro aereo

All'improvviso calò
nascondendosi dietro il muro cadente
di nuvole color indigo spinte
dall'ultimo raggio
Cadde un momento silenzioso d'oscurità

Attraversammo la soglia
Satura d'oro l'alba scintillante
Si dissolse svelando
il grande scudo del Sole
che permeò le finestre dell'aereo

Il sogno che non ce la fece
scivolò giù il globo terrestre
tra il rosso e l'oro
del tramonto e dell'alba
Era nato un nuovo ordinario giorno

prima che un uomo uccidesse con un uomo
aerei ed edifici
pieni di uomini

settembre 2001

Antes de que un ser humano matara con otro humano

Vertientes de rojo saturaban
los vendajes de nubes
y palidecían al ir revelando
un gran escudo de Sol
El esplendor envolvió nuestro avión

De repente se esfumó
oculto tras el derrumbe
de nubes índigo impulsadas
por el último rayo de sol
Callado momento de tinieblas

Cruzamos el umbral
El alba brillante saturada de oro
se desvaneció revelando
el gran escudo de Sol
Impregnó las ventanillas del avión

El sueño que no llegó
se deslizó bajo la esfera de la Tierra
entre el rojo y el oro
del ocaso-aurora
Un nuevo día como tantos nació

antes de que un ser humano matara con otro humano
aviones y edificios
llenos de seres humanos

Septiembre 2001

Avant qu'un humain ait tué avec un humain

Des débordements de rouge ont saturé
des pansements de nuages
et se sont pâlis en découvrant
un grand bouclier de Soleil
La luminosité a capturé notre avion

D'un coup il a décliné
s'est caché derrière le mur s'effondrant
de nuages l'indigo saisi
par le dernier rayon
Moment silencieux d'obscurité est tombé

Nous avons traversé le seuil
L'aube scintillante saturée d'or
s'est dissous en découvrant
le grand bouclier de Soleil
Il se répandait sur les fenêtres de l'avion

Le rêve qui n'a pas réussi
s'est glissé sur the ballon de la Terre
entre le rouge et l'or
de la couchée et la levée du soleil
Un nouveau jour ordinaire est né

avant qu'un humain ait tué avec un humain
des avions et des buildings
pleins d'humains

septembre 2001

Bevor ein Mensch machte Menschenmord

Rot durchtränkte Flecken
bandagierte Wolken
und das matte Erscheinen
eines großen Sonnenballs
dessen Helle unser Flugzeug versank

Plötzliches Verschwinden
hinter einer sinkenden Mauer
von blauen Wolken sichtbar
im letzten Strahl
stiller Moment der einsetzenden Dunkelheit

Wir überquerten die Schwelle
zum gold-schimmernden Morgen
aus dem Dämmer erschien
der große Sonnenball
der die Flugzeugfenster erhellte

Der nicht verwirklichte Traum
fiel auf den Erdball
zwischen das Rot und das Gold
von sinkender und steigender Sonne
Ein neuer Tag erblickte das Licht

bevor ein Mensch machte Menschenmord
Flugzeuge und Gebäude
voller Menschen

September 2001

Se aika ennen kuin ihmiset tappoivat toisiensa

Punaiset vuodot läpimärkänä
pilvet kuin sidoteet
ja kalpeutta paljastamassa
sitä ison auringon kilveä
tämän loiste otti lentokoneen vangiksi

Yhtäkkiä se heikentyi
piilotteli kaatuvan seinän takana
siniset pilvet ajettu sisään
viimeisellä säteellä
Hiljainen hetki vaihtui pimeytyyn.

Ylittimme kynnyksen
aamu tuottaa loistavaa kultaa
sulautui ja paljastui
tämän ison auringon kilven
se imeytyi lentokoneen ikkunaan

Unelma joka epäonnistui
maapallo liukui alas
auringonlaskun ja auringonnousun
punaisen ja kullan vällissä
Uusi tavallinen päivä syntyi

Se aika ennen kuin ihmiset tappoivat toiisensa
lentokoneita ja rakennuksia
täynä ihmisiä

syyskuu 2001

Mielőtt egy ember egy emberrel ölt

Kicsurgott vörös tócsák
a felhők géz kötéseibe itatodtak
és elhalványodtak kibontva
a Nap nagy pajzsát
A fény hatalmába vette repülőnket

Hirtelen gyengült el
elbújt az indigo felhő mögött
amit az utolsó sugár
taszitott be
Sötétség csendes pillanata hullott le

Mi átléptünk a küszöbön
Arannyal-itatott villogó hajnal
feloldododt kibontva
a Nap nagy pajzsát
Beleszivárgott a repülő ablakaiba

Az álom aminek nem sikerült
az lecsuszott a Föld labdájáról
az alkony és a napfelmente
vörös és arany árnyalata közt
Egy közönséges nap kezdödött el

mielőtt egy ember egy emberrel ölt
repülőkkel és épületekkel emberekkel tele

szeptember 2001

POEM EIGHT

Awareness

rushing
with the river
swayed
on the lake's waves
tossed
by the white water stream
hauled by a hurricane
onto enraged
waters
of the sea rising over the banks
holding on
by the truth of salt

Świadomość

spiesząca
bystrą rzeką
kołysana
falami jeziora
wirująca
rwącym potokiem
przerzucana huraganem
na występujące z brzegów
wody wzburzonego morza
utrzymująca się
na powierzchni
prawdą soli

Сознание

несомое
быстрой рекой
колышимое
волнами озера
кружимое
бурным потоком
бросаемое
ураганом
в вышедшие из берегов
воды
взбешенного моря
удерживаемое на поверхности
правдой соли

Consapevolezza

scorrendo
con il fiume
cullata
sulle onde del lago
scossa
dal fiume dalle acque bianche
scaraventata da un uragano
nella furia
delle acque
del mare che oltrepassa gli argini
mi aggrappo
alla verità di sale

Conciencia

corriendo
con el río
remecida
en las ondas del lago
a tumbos
por los rápidos
arrastrada por el huracán
a las furiosas
aguas
de ese mar que se desborda
me aferro
a la verdad de la sal

Conscience

se precipitant
avec le fleuve
ondulant
sur les vagues du lac
secouée
par le flot des eaux vives
halée par l'ouragan
sur les eaux
en rage
de la mer qui se déborde sur les rives
tenant bon
par la vérité du sel

Bewusstsein

rauschend
mit dem Fluss
gewiegt
auf den Wellen des Sees
umhergeschüttelt
vom Wildwasserstrom
geworfen von einem Wirbelsturm
auf wütende
Wasser
der See über die Ufer herziehend
sich fest haltend
an der Wahrheit des Salzes

Tietoisuus

kiirehtiä
joen kanssa
keinuttelin
järven aalloilla
heitetty
valkoisen veden virralla
viskattu
hurrikaanin toimesta
raivistuneille
vesille
meri
nousemassa pengerien yli
pitämällä kiinni
suolan totuudesta

Tudat

robog
a folyóval
dobálja
a habzó folyó
roham
egy forgószel
átlenditi
örjöngő vizekbe
partokon átcsapó
tengerbe
csak a só igazsága
tartja meg

POEM NINE

Settles in the Heart

A little green ball
Rolls on rolls on
Tossed like a prize
At a toddler's feet
Plays green on green
Touches the fingers
Leaves too soon
The longing hands

Rolls on rolls on
A winding ribbon
Sinks into darkness
Revives in dawn
Sparkles the braids
Of a teenage girl
Runs down in tears
Of a woman's defeats

Rolls on rolls on
In happiness glows
Dims in grief
Returns in wisdom
Settles in the heart
Free like the heart
Keeps it from doubting
A little green ball

Rolls on rolls on

W sercu zamieszka

Toczy się toczy
Zielona kulka
Rzucona dziecku
Jak los pod nogi
Zagra zielenią
Popieści palce
Przemknie dotykiem
Po pragnieniu rąk

Toczy się toczy
Po wstęgach wije
Zapada w ciemność
Powraca w zorzy
Błyśnie w warkoczach
Młodej dziewczyny
Spłynie ze łzami
Dojrzałych już strat

Toczy się toczy
Rozbłyśnie szczęściem
Zgaśnie żałobą
Głębią powróci
W sercu zamieszka
Wolna jak serce
Nie da mu zwątpić
Zielona kulka

Toczy się toczy

Встанет в сердце

Катится катится
Мячик зеленый
Брошен под ноги
Как приз малышу
пальцев коснется
Боком зеленым
Вдруг ускользнет
Из жадных рук

Катится, катится
Вьется по ленте
Падает в мрак
Воскресает в заре
Блесткой сверкает
В девичьих косах
Струится слезами
Женских утрат

Катится катится
В радости яркий
В горе поблекший
Мудрым вернется
И встанет в сердце
Как сердце свободный
Изгонит горечь
Мячик зеленый

Катится катится

Si Deposita nel Cuore

Una piccola palla verde
Rotola rotola
Lanciata come un premio
Ai piedi di un bimbetto
Gioca verde su verde
Tocca le dita
Lascia troppo in fretta
Le mani protese

Rotola rotola
Un nastro serpeggiante
Affonda nell'oscurità
Si rianima all'alba
Fa scintillare le treccie
Di una ragazzina
Scivola sulle lacrime
Delle sconfitte d'una donna

Rotola rotola
Risplende di felicità
Affievolisce col dolore
Ritorna nella saggezza
Si deposita nel cuore
Libera come il cuore
Gli impedisce di dubitare
Una piccola palla verde

Rotola rotola

Se queda en el corazón

Rueda y rueda
Una canica verde
Lanzada como un premio
A los pies de un chiquillo
Juguetea verde en el verdor
Roza los dedos
Y pronto abandona
Las ávidas manos

Rueda y rueda
Serpentina
Se hunde en la noche
Renace al alba
Centellea en las trenzas
De una quinceañera
Se derrama en lágrimas
Infortunios de mujer

Rueda y rueda
Resplandece en la dicha
Se apaga en la pena
Es sabia al regreso
Se queda en el corazón
Libre como el corazón
No lo deja dudar
Una canica verde

Rueda y rueda

Se pose dans le cœur

Un petit ballon vert
Roule et roule
Lancé comme un prix
Aux pieds d'un bambin
Joue vert sur vert
Touche aux doigts
Part trop tôt
Des mains envieuses

Roule et roule
Un ruban sinueux
Coule dans l'obscurité
Se ranime à l'aube
Fait étinceler les nattes
D'une adolescente
Coule en larmes
Des échecs d'une femme

Roule et roule
Dans le bonheur luit
Baisse dans le chagrin
Revient en sagesse
Se pose dans le cœur
Libre comme le cœur
L'empêche de douter
Un petit ballon vert

Roule et roule

Sinkt ins Herz

Ein kleiner grüner Ball
Der rollt und rollt
Geworfen wie eine Beute
Einem Kleinen vor die Füße
Spielt grün auf grün
Berührt die Finger
Entschlüpft zu früh
Den sehnsüchtigen Händchen

Rollt und rollt
Ein verschlungenes Band
Entschwindet im Dunkel
Wiederbelebt am Morgen
Glitzert in den Zöpfen
Eines Teenager Mädchens
Kullernde Tränen
Einer niedergeschlagenen Frau

Rollt und rollt
Leuchtet im Glück
Wird dunkel in Trauer
Kehrt wieder in Weisheit
Sinkt ins Herz
Frei wie das Herz
Beseitigt jeden Zweifel
Ein kleiner grüner Ball

Der rollt und rollt

Asettuen sydämmeen

Pieni vihreä pallo
Pyörii ja pyörii eteenpäin
Heitetty kuin palkinto
Kohti lapsen jalkojaan
Pelaa vihreätä vihreällä
Koskettaa sormiansa
Pallo lähtee liian aikaisin
Ei saanut käteen pallo

Pyörii ja pyörii eteenpäin
Kiemurteleva nauha
Uppoaa pimeyteen
Herättäen aamun koitossa
Hiusletit ovat helmeilevät
Teini-ikuisella tytöllä
Itkeän hän juoksee alaspäin
Kun on naisen tappio

Pyörii ja pyörii eteenpäin
Onnellisuus hehkuu
Himmenee surussa
Tulee viisaudessa takaisin
Asettuen sydämmeen
Vapaa kuin sydän
Joka estää sitä epäilemästä
Pieni vihreä pallo

Pyörii ja pyärii eteenpäin

Letelepszik a szívben

Gurul a kis zöld golyó
gurul tovább és tovább
Mint egy nyeremény
Totyogó gyerekhez dobva
Játszik zölded a zöldön
Érintve az ujjhegyeket
Hamar tovabb fut
Az áhítozó kezekből

Gurul tovább és tovább
A kacskaringós szallag
Sötétbe merül
Hajnalban életre kel
Szikrázik egy tizenéves
Lányka copfján
Sirva fut le egy asszony
Vereségein

Gurul tovább és tovább
Bolgogságban fénylik
Búban megszürkül
Bölcsen visszatér
Letelepszik a szívben
Szabadon mint a szív
Kétségektől megóvja
A kis zöld golyó

Gurul tovább és tovább

Biographical Notes

Lidia Kosk, a poet, storyteller, educator, humanitarian. Author of thirteen books of poetry and prose, and two anthologies. Her collaboration with Danuta E. Kosk-Kosicka, resulted in two bilingual volumes: *Niedosyt/Reshapings* (2003) and *Słodka woda, słona woda/Sweet Water, Salt Water* (2009). The latter was translated into Japanese by Hiroko Tsuji and Izumi Nakamura, and published in Japan in 2016. Among her recent books are: *Szklana góra/Glass Mountain* (Komograf, 2017 & 2019) and *Meadows of Memory: Poetry and Prose by Lidia Kosk* (Apprentice House, 2019), both edited and translated by Danuta E. Kosk-Kosicka; and *Konie bez skrzydeł* (LSW, 2021).

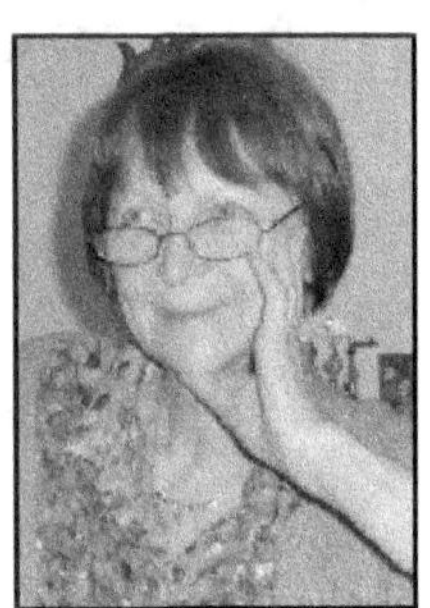

Danuta E. Kosk-Kosicka is the author of *Oblige the Light* (CityLit Press, 2015), winner of Clarinda Harriss Poetry Prize, and *Face Half-Illuminated* (Apprentice House, 2015). She has translated four books by the Polish poet Lidia Kosk as well as poems by other Polish- and English-language poets, including Josephine Jacobsen, Lucille Clifton, Linda Pastan, and Grace Cavalieri. Recently she's edited Thirty-three translations of a poem by Lidia Kosk, contributing her English translation of "From the Window of My Apartment." Poetry Translations Editor at *Loch Raven Review*, she grew up in Poland and now lives in Maryland, USA. For more, see danutakk.wordpress.com.

Natalia Romanova, born in Moscow, Russia, has a BA, MA, and a PhD in second language acquisition and pedagogy, and an MA in translation. She has translated poetry and texts of various genres from English, Russian, French, and Polish. Her translation of the title poem into Russian appeared in *Szklana góra/Glass Mountain* by Lidia Kosk (Komograf, Poland, 2017). Translated into Russian "From the Window of My Apartment," recently featured in *Loch Raven Review* in Thirty-three translations of a poem by Lidia Kosk. Currently teaches at The George Washington University.

Sabine Pascarelli earned her degree in German language and literature at Dortmund University. A published poet, children's literature author, translator of English, German and Italian; her work includes *The Alchemy of Grief* by Emily Ferrara, Bordighera Poetry Award 2007 winner; *Repubblica* by Dr. J.H. Beall, (Toad Hall Press); *Cosa farei per amore* by Grace Cavalieri (The Bunny & the Crocodile Press). Contributed to Lidia Kosk's *Szklana Góra/Glass Mountain* and to Thirty-three translations of a poem by Lidia Kosk, featuring "From the Window of My Apartment." Resides in Florence, Italy.

Patricia Bejarano Fisher was born in Colombia, has a BA in French Literature from the University of Pittsburgh and an MA in Linguistics from the State University of New York at Buffalo. She is a translator, developer of language learning materials, and language instructor. Co-translator of Maria Teresa Ogliastri's *South Pole/Polo Sur* (Settlement House, 2011). Her work has appeared in *Knocking on the Door of the White House: Latino Poets in Washington DC* (Zozobra, 2017), and Laura Shovan's *The Last Fifth Grade of Emerson Elementary* (WLB, 2016). Translated into Spanish the title poem in *Szklana góra/Glass Mountain* by Lidia Kosk (2017). Contributed to Thirty-three translations of a poem by Lidia Kosk, featuring "From the Window of My Apartment."

Keith Cohen is a writer and translator who lived and taught for five years in France. He has published a novel (*Natural Settings*), and his stories have appeared in *The Paris Review* and *The Iowa Review*. A former professor of comparative literature, he is the author of *Film and Fiction*, and related non-fiction works, as well as translations by Hélène Cixous ("The Laugh of the Medusa") and the collective work *A History of Virility*. His latest translation of a poem into French appeared in *Szklana góra/Glass Mountain* by Lidia Kosk. He is currently translating poems by the Haitian poet Denizé Lauture.

Peter Beicken has published versions of his work in German and translated poetry, prose, and essays into English. He published widely on Franz Kafka, Ingeborg Bachmann, Anna Seghers, and filmmaker Wim Wenders. He authored several books of poetry in German. Having edited two magazines for literature in German in the U.S., he also has published many poems, prose pieces, and essays in journals and anthologies, predominantly in German and in English as well. His poems and translations appeared in German-language poets *LRR* Vol. 16.

Irmeli Kuehnel, translates Finnish, German, Swedish, Norwegian, Danish and Dutch into English. Authored two scholarly studies on German medieval epics. Genealogy translations in Finnish, Norwegian, and German. PhD focused on Medieval Studies in German. Published a dual-language Swedish-English work "The Swedes in America," authored in 1885, that includes songs and poems that speak to Scandinavian immigration. Translated into Finnish "From the Window of My Apartment," featured in *Loch Raven Review* in Thirty-three translations of a poem by Lidia Kosk.

Paul Sohar (d. 2023) wrote and published in every genre, including seventeen volumes of translations, the latest being T*he Conscience of Trees* (Ragged Sky, 2018) and *The Refugee* (Syergebooks, 2019). His own poetry: *Homing Poems* (Iniquity Press, 2006), *The Wayward Orchard* (Wordrunner Press Prize winner, 2011), and *In Sun's Shadow* (Ragged Sky Press, 2020). Prose works: *True Tales of a Fictitious Spy* (Synergebooks, 2006) and a collection of one-act plays from One Act Depot (Saskatoon, Canada, 2014). Magazines: *Agni, Gargoyle, Rattle,* etc. Published Transylvania's Hungarian poets in *LRR* Vol. 14.

www.ingramcontent.com/pod-product-compliance
Lightning Source LLC
LaVergne TN
LVHW010840120826
845149LV00017B/3334